WRITING
WHIRLWIND

Linda Polon

Scott, Foresman and Company
Glenview, Illinois   London

Good Year Books

are available for preschool through grade 12 and for every basic curriculum subject plus many enrichment areas. For more Good Year Books, contact your local bookseller or educational dealer. For a complete catalog with information about other Good Year Books, please write:

Good Year Books
Department GYB
1900 East Lake Avenue
Glenview, Illinois 60025

ISBN 0-673-18310-6

5 6-MAL-91 90

Dedication

- To my editor, a friend who has faith in my writing ability

- To my loving, supportive parents, Hal and Edie Wolff

- To Brooke Barton, who has helped me during rough times

- To Dena Finley, a lady who never stops smiling

The Purpose and Use of This Book

The activities in this book begin with sentence completion, progress to the writing of simple sentences, and end with activities that enable students to express more complete thoughts. The activities are focused to foster creative thinking and free writing. The fact that there are no "wrong" answers contributes to an atmosphere of inventiveness and accomplishment.

Each activity appears on an individual, perforated worksheet for easy reproduction. The worksheets can be used separately or grouped by subject matter and used as center work.

A child has a vivid and creative imagination. The author of this book has successfully enhanced this attribute through the use of these activities. You can too.

Table of Contents

Fortune Telling

A fortune teller reads lines on the palm of your hand and tells your fortune. Pretend a fortune teller is reading the lines on this hand. The hand belongs to you. What would you want the fortune teller to say about you?

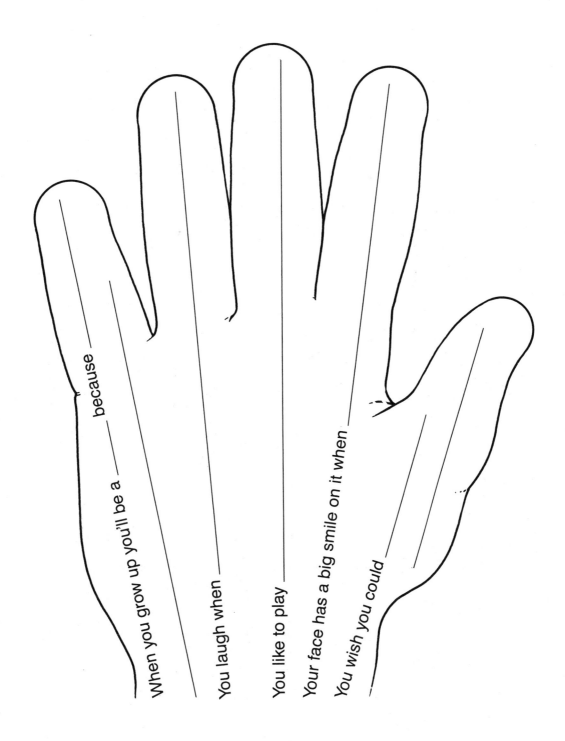

When you grow up you'll be a _____ because

You laugh when

You like to play

Your face has a big smile on it when

You wish you could

Fortune Telling

A fortune teller reads lines on the palm of your hand and tells your fortune. Pretend a fortune teller is reading the lines on this hand. The hand belongs to you. What would you want the fortune teller to say about you?

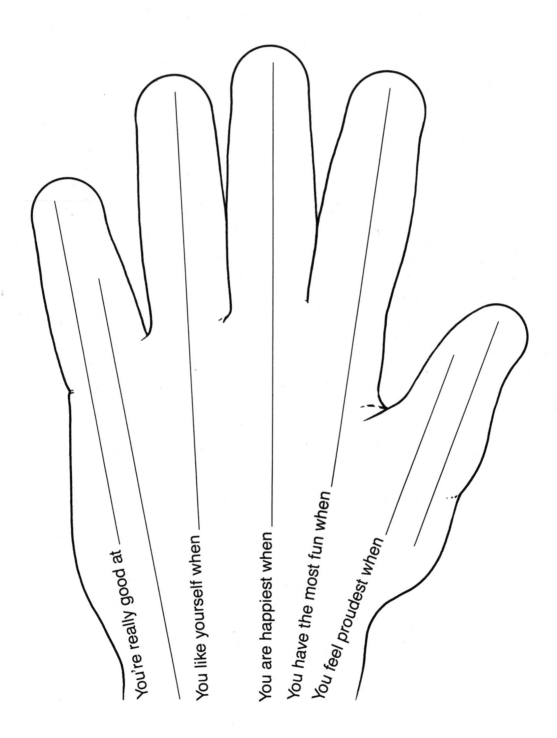

You're really good at _____

You like yourself when _____

You are happiest when _____

You have the most fun when _____

You feel proudest when _____

Fortune Telling

A fortune teller reads lines on the palm of your hand and tells your fortune. Pretend a fortune teller is reading the lines on this hand. The hand belongs to you. What would you want the fortune teller to say about you?

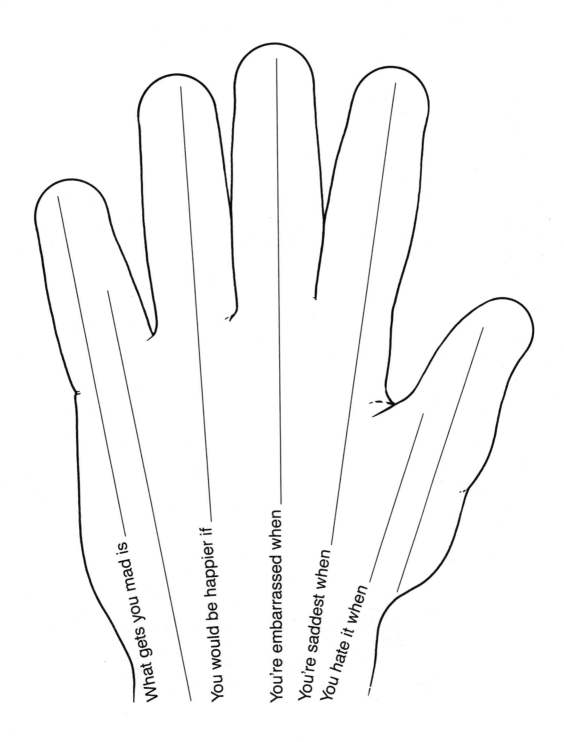

What gets you mad is

You would be happier if

You're embarrassed when

You're saddest when

You hate it when

Fortune Telling

Pretend you can read a crystal ball. A crystal ball tells things about people. Look into the crystal ball to find out the answers to the problems you may have. How could these problems be solved?

1. You don't like the clothes your parents pick out for you._____

_____

_____

2. You didn't do your homework and do not know what to tell the teacher.

_____

_____

_____

3. Your best friend tattletales on you._____

_____

_____

Fortune Telling

A fortune teller sometimes reads tea leaves to tell your fortune. Read the tea leaves. Write a question you'd like answered by a fortune teller. For example: next to *school* you might write a question like *How can I play hop scotch better?*

1. school  _____
   _____
   _____
   _____

2. a friend 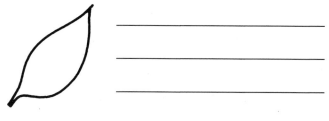 _____
   _____
   _____
   _____

3. parents _____
   _____
   _____
   _____
   _____

4. a brother
   or a sister  _____
   _____
   _____
   _____

You, the Space Creature

Pretend you are a creature from outer space.

1. Name your planet. _____

2. Tell your name and describe what you look like. _____

_____

_____

_____

Draw a picture of yourself.

_____

3. Describe where you live. _____

_____

4. On the back of this page draw a picture of your family standing in front of where you live.

You, the Space Creature

Pretend you are a creature from outer space.

1. Why do you want to go to the planet earth?_____

_____

_____

_____

2. How are you going to travel to earth?_____

_____

_____

3. Draw a picture of the spacecraft you are going to travel on to earth.

_____

You, the Space Creature

You have landed on planet earth.

1. Where did you land on earth? _____

_____

Draw a picture of where you landed on earth.

```
┌─────────────────────────────────────────────┐
│                                             │
│                                             │
│                                             │
│                                             │
│                                             │
│                                             │
│                                             │
│                                             │
│                                             │
│                                             │
│                                             │
│                                             │
└─────────────────────────────────────────────┘
```

2. How did you feel when you first landed on earth? _____

_____

_____

3. What does someone from earth look like? _____

_____

_____

4. What is the first question you wanted to ask an earthling? _____

_____

_____

5. On the back of this page draw a picture of the first earthling you saw.

You, the Space Creature

1. Write to your home planet and tell what you saw on earth.

    1. _____

    2. _____

    3. _____

    4. _____

2. Draw a picture of what earthlings do that looks funny to you.

Tell what they do.

_____

_____

_____

_____

_____

_____

You, the Space Creature

You have a camera. What are your favorite places on earth to take pictures of? You are going to take these pictures back to your planet. Draw each picture and tell about each snapshot.

1.

_____

_____

_____

_____

_____

_____

_____

2.

_____

_____

_____

_____

_____

_____

_____

_____

_____

You, the Space Creature

You can bring some things back to your planet. These things show your space creature friends what earth is like. What will you bring? Draw the things in the spaceship and tell about them.

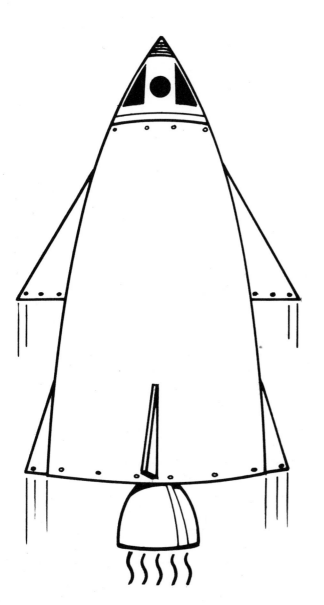

_____

_____

_____

_____

_____

_____

_____

_____

_____

_____

_____

_____

You, the Space Creature

You are taking one earthling back to your planet. Draw a picture of the earthling and tell why you chose this person.

_____
_____
_____
_____
_____
_____

Fast-Food Restaurants

Fast-food restaurants try to get the most customers by giving fast service, the best food, and contests.

1. What fast-food restaurants have you eaten at? _____

_____

_____

2. What restaurants are your favorites? List them in order. Your most favorite one is first. Write why you like each one.

    1. _____   _____

                                                     _____

    2. _____   _____

                                                     _____

    3. _____   _____

                                                     _____

    4. _____   _____

                                                     _____

Draw a picture of your most favorite fast-food restaurant.

Fast-Food Restaurants

Make believe you own a fast-food restaurant. How can you make it the best?

1. What would you call it? _____

2. Draw a picture of the outside of your restaurant and tell what it looks like.

_____

_____

_____

3. Draw a picture of the inside of your restaurant and tell what it looks like.

_____

_____

_____

Fast-Food Restaurants

To bring in customers, McDonalds has a character named Ronald McDonald. Burger King has a slogan *HAVE IT YOUR WAY.* What character and slogan can you make up for your restaurant?

1. Name your character. _____

What does he or she look like? _____

_____

Draw a picture of your character.

_____

2. What is your slogan for your restaurant?_____

_____

3. Some restaurants sell you drinks and let you keep the glass it comes in. This is

called a giveaway. What will be your giveaway? _____

_____

Fast-Food Restaurants

Draw a poster that tells about your restaurant. The poster should make people come to your restaurant. Tell why the poster will make people come to your restaurant.

_____

_____

_____

_____

_____

Fast-Food Restaurants

Draw a picture of the food you'll serve in your restaurant. Give the
name, tell the price, and why it is special.

	Name of food	Price	Why it's so special
	_____	_____	_____
			_____
			_____
			_____
			_____
			_____
			_____

	Name of food	Price	Why it's so special
	_____	_____	_____
			_____
			_____
			_____
			_____
			_____
			_____

Fast-Food Restaurants

Contests bring in customers. Children and grown-ups like to win
things. Tell about the contest you are having at your restaurant.
Draw a poster that tells about it.

1. _____

_____

_____

_____

From *Writing Whirlwind,* Copyright © 1986 Scott, Foresman and Company

Vacations

Vacations are when you go on trips.

1. What trips have you taken with your family? _____

_____

_____

2. Name one place you'd like to visit on a trip. _____

_____

_____

3. Why do you want to go to this place? _____

_____

_____

4. Draw pictures in the suitcase of the things you'd take along on your trip.

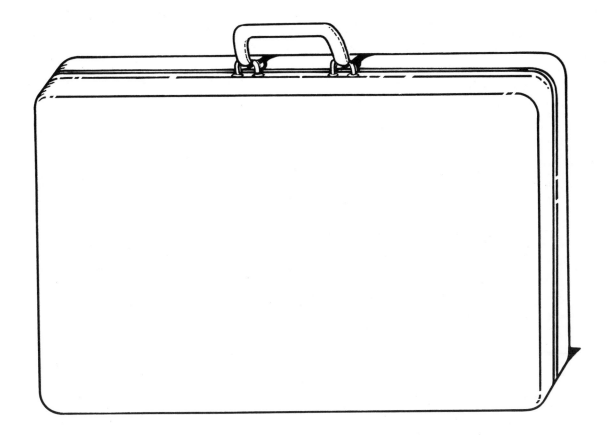

Vacations

Draw the front of a postcard you would send to a friend on your trip.
The front of a postcard is a picture of your vacation spot.
Tell about your vacation spot.

_____

_____

_____

Write a postcard to a friend and tell him or her what you're doing on
your trip. Remember to color the stamp and write in the address.

Dear _____ **,**

20

Vacations

Sometimes people keep a diary of the fun things they do on vacations.
Pretend you kept a diary and wrote about the first two days of your trip.
Draw a picture of what you did too.

FIRST DAY

Dear Diary. _____

_____

_____

_____

_____

_____

_____

SECOND DAY

Dear Diary. _____

_____

_____

_____

_____

_____

_____

Vacations

Think up a make-believe vacation place you'd like to visit.

1. What would you want to call it? _____

_____

2. What fun things would you like to have for children to do at this vacation place? ____

_____

3. Design a poster advertising your vacation place. Write why children should visit it.

Picture Taking

With a camera you can take pictures of yourself, family, and friends.

1. Take a picture of your pet doing something with you. Tell about the picture.

_____

_____

_____

_____

_____

2. Take a picture of your teacher. Tell about the picture.

_____

_____

_____

_____

_____

3. Take a picture of your favorite place in your home, backyard, or neighborhood. Tell about the picture.

_____

_____

_____

_____

_____

Picture Taking

With a camera you can take pictures of things at your school.
Tell about the picture.

1. Take a picture of your favorite place at school. Tell about the picture.

_____

_____

_____

_____

_____

2. Have a friend take a picture of you enjoying your favorite thing at school.
Tell about the picture.

_____

_____

_____

_____

_____

3. Take a picture of the funniest thing you have seen at school. Tell about the picture.

_____

_____

_____

_____

_____

Picture Taking

Pictures help us remember the past and the things we have done or felt.

1. Have a friend take a picture of when you felt your best.
Tell about the picture, what you were doing, and why you felt so good.

_____

_____

_____

_____

_____

_____

_____

_____

2. Have a friend take a picture of you when you felt very important.
Tell about the picture and why you felt important.

_____

_____

_____

_____

_____

_____

_____

_____

School

Think about the school you go to now. Would you like to make some changes to it?

1. If you could rename your school, what would you call it? _____

_____

2. Draw a picture of the outside of the way you'd like your school to look like.
Tell about the picture.

```




```

_____

_____

_____

_____

School

Most of a school day is spent in the classroom. Do you like your classroom?

1. Draw a picture of your classroom and tell about the picture.

_____

_____

_____

_____

_____

_____

_____

_____

2. If you were to make changes in your classroom, what would they look like? Draw a picture of the new classroom and tell about the picture.

_____

_____

_____

_____

_____

_____

_____

_____

School

1. Draw a picture of your teacher and tell why you like him or her.

_____

_____

_____

_____

_____

_____

_____

_____

2. Write down the things you'd like to learn from your teacher.
Tell why?

1. _____   _____

2. _____   _____

3. _____   _____

4. _____   _____

_____

_____

School

What if you had a new building at your school? How would you like it to be used?

1. Draw a picture of this new building and tell about the picture.

_____

_____

_____

_____

_____

_____

_____

_____

2. Draw a picture of the inside of this new building and tell what is inside.

_____

_____

_____

_____

_____

_____

_____

_____

School

Each school has a yard. What does yours look like?

1. Draw a picture of your schoolyard and tell about the picture.

[picture box]

_____

_____

_____

_____

_____

_____

_____

_____

2. If you had the chance to change your schoolyard, what changes would you make? Draw a picture of this new schoolyard and tell about the picture.

[picture box]

_____

_____

_____

_____

_____

_____

_____

_____

School

Most schools have a cafeteria. What do you think of yours?

1. If you had a choice, what kinds of food would you like to be served in your cafeteria?

    1. _____

    2. _____

    3. _____

    4. _____

    5. _____

2. Draw a picture of a new cafeteria, one that is more comfortable than the one you have now. Tell about the changes you would make.

_____

_____

_____

_____

_____

_____

My New Home

1. How would you feel if you had to move from the home you live in now?

_____

_____

_____

2. Draw a picture of your favorite place in your home and tell about it.

_____

_____

_____

_____

My New Home

Pretend you're in a new home.

1. Draw a picture of your new home and tell about it.

_____

_____

_____

2. Draw a picture of your new room and tell about it.

_____

_____

_____

My New Home

1. You will have new friends in your neighborhood. How are you going to meet them?

_____

_____

_____

2. Draw a picture of your new friends and tell about them.

_____

_____

_____

_____

3. What would you like to play with your new friends?_____

_____

_____

_____

My New Home

1. Draw a picture of your new school and tell about it.

_____

_____

_____

2. What would make you feel happy the first day of school?_____

_____

3. Draw a picture of your new classroom and teacher. Tell about them.

_____

_____

_____

My Own TV Show

Do you like television shows? Now is your chance to make your own show.

1. Name two of your favorite TV shows. Why do you like them?

TV Shows	**Why you like them**
1. _____	_____
	_____
	_____
	_____
2. _____	_____
	_____
	_____
	_____

2. If you were making up your own TV show, what would you call it?

_____

3. What would your show be about? _____

_____

_____

_____

My Own TV Show

Name two people (characters) in your TV show. Tell something about each one (what they do). Draw a picture of each one.

_____

_____

_____

_____

_____

_____

_____

_____

_____

_____

_____

_____

_____

_____

_____

My Own TV Show

In the squares write what the people on your TV show may say to each other in a scene. Don't forget to draw the people and the background setting.

Toys

All children play with toys. Think of some of the toys you have played with.

1. What toys did you play with when you were younger? _____

_____

_____

2. What is your favorite toy now and why? _____

_____

_____

3. Combine two toys together to make one. Draw a picture of it and tell about it.

_____

_____

_____

_____

_____

_____

_____

_____

_____

_____

_____

_____

Toys

1. What kind of toy would you make up for a child under five years old? Draw a picture of it and tell about it.

<table>
<tr><td></td><td>_____</td></tr>
<tr><td></td><td>_____</td></tr>
<tr><td></td><td>_____</td></tr>
<tr><td></td><td>_____</td></tr>
<tr><td></td><td>_____</td></tr>
<tr><td></td><td>_____</td></tr>
<tr><td></td><td>_____</td></tr>
<tr><td></td><td>_____</td></tr>
</table>

2. Draw a picture of a toy you'd make for a child your own age and tell about it.

<table>
<tr><td></td><td>_____</td></tr>
<tr><td></td><td>_____</td></tr>
<tr><td></td><td>_____</td></tr>
<tr><td></td><td>_____</td></tr>
<tr><td></td><td>_____</td></tr>
<tr><td></td><td>_____</td></tr>
<tr><td></td><td>_____</td></tr>
<tr><td></td><td>_____</td></tr>
</table>

Toys

Draw a picture of a toy the people listed below would like. Write why you chose each one for them.

1. Your best friend

```
┌─────────────────────────┐        _____
│                         │
│                         │        _____
│                         │
│                         │        _____
│                         │
│                         │        _____
│                         │
│                         │        _____
└─────────────────────────┘
```

2. Your brother

```
┌─────────────────────────┐        _____
│                         │
│                         │        _____
│                         │
│                         │        _____
│                         │
│                         │        _____
│                         │
│                         │        _____
└─────────────────────────┘
```

3. Your sister

```
┌─────────────────────────┐        _____
│                         │
│                         │        _____
│                         │
│                         │        _____
│                         │
│                         │        _____
│                         │
│                         │        _____
└─────────────────────────┘
```

Toys

Children like video games.
Draw a picture of two of your favorite video games and tell why you
like them.

1.

```
┌─────────────────────────┐     _____
│                         │
│                         │     _____
│                         │
│                         │     _____
│                         │
│                         │     _____
│                         │
│                         │     _____
└─────────────────────────┘
```

```
┌─────────────────────────┐     _____
│                         │
│                         │     _____
│                         │
│                         │     _____
│                         │
│                         │     _____
│                         │
│                         │     _____
└─────────────────────────┘
```

2. Make up your own video game. Draw a picture of it and tell about it.

```
┌──────────────────────┐     _____
│                      │
│                      │     _____
│                      │
│                      │     _____
│                      │
│                      │     _____
│                      │
│                      │     _____
└──────────────────────┘
```

Changing Places

Would you like to change places with a character in a book, a movie or
TV star, a cartoon character, or a real person? Think of a situation or
problem the character may be involved with. Describe what you would
do in this character's situation. What would you do if you were . . .

1. Dorothy *(Wizard of Oz)* _____

_____

_____

2. The President of the United States _____

_____

_____

3. Your favorite TV star _____

_____

_____

4. Jack *(Jack in the Beanstalk)* _____

_____

_____

5. Santa Claus _____

_____

_____

6. E.T. _____

_____

_____

Changing Places

Have you ever thought of changing places with an animal or
something that is not alive? Tell what you would do if you were one of
these things.

1. A lion _____

_____

_____

2. A telephone _____

_____

_____

3. A car _____

_____

_____

4. A monkey _____

_____

_____

5. A TV set _____

_____

_____

6. A parrot _____

_____

_____

7. An elephant _____

_____

_____